To My Grandchildren, My Inspiration.
- Giddo M.

Text Copyright © 2022 by Mohamed El Mouelhi.
Illustrations Copyright © 2022 by Hossam El Mouelhi and Donia Farouk.

All Rights Reserved. No part of this book may be reproduced, transmitted, or stored in an information retrieval system in any form or by any means, graphic, electronic, or mechanical, including photocopying, taping, and recording, without prior written permission from the publisher.

جميع الحقوق محفوظة.

ISBN 978-1-7357701-6-1

First edition 2022

Published by Honey Elm Books LLC
www.HoneyElmBooks.com

Ibrahim PBUH
إبراهيم عليه السلام

Editing: Noha Elmouelhi

Artistic Preparation: Hossam El Mouelhi - Donia Farouk

تحرير: نهى المويلحي

الإعداد الفني: حسام المويلحي - دنيا فاروق

Prophet Ibrahim was from the descendants of Prophet Nuh.
He grew up in a society that worshiped idols and statues. His father was an idol maker.
Ibrahim used to watch his father craft these statues, then give them names, and then worship them as gods.

جاء سيدنا إبراهيم بعد سيدنا نوح، ونشأ في مجتمع يعبد الأصنام والتماثيل، فقد كان أبوه أحد صناع هذه التماثيل، وترعرع إبراهيم وهو يرى أباه ينحت هذه التماثيل ويشكلها ثم بعد ذلك يعطونها أسماء ويقومون بعبادتها على أنها آلهة.

However, Ibrahim was not convinced and he questioned the ability of a statue crafted by his father out of clay to have any sort of power or potential to be a god.

He started his religious journey wondering about the identity of a real God with absolute power and Creator of the universe.

ولكن إبراهيم لم يقتنع بهذا الوضع وتساءل كيف يمكن لصنم يقوم أبوه بصنعه لا حول ولا قوة له أن يكون إلها يعبده الناس! وبدأ رحلة البحث والتفكر في الإله الحقيقى والخالق لكل شئ.

One night, he saw a faraway star shining in the sky and was impressed. He wondered if this could be God? Then, he saw the moon in the sky, bigger and brighter than any star and wondered if this could be God? However, when the moon disappeared, he realized this could not be God and asked for guidance from an Almighty Creator.

وفى أحد الليالى رأى نجم بعيد منير فى السماء، وأُعجب إبراهيم به وظن أنه هو الله، ولكنه بعدها رأى القمر بازغاً فى السماء وكان نوره أقوى وحجمه أكبر من كل النجوم، فأقتنع إبراهيم أن القمر هو الإله الواجب عبادته، ولكن عندما غاب القمر قال هذا لا يمكن أن يكون هو الله،

وسأل الله أن يهديه الى الصواب.

In the morning, he saw the sun shining and spreading its light and warmth on Earth. It appeared even bigger and brighter than the moon. He told himself this must be the God I have been searching for.

He continued thinking about the sun until it set and it too disappeared! He was surprised – surely a God would not disappear at night. This can't be, he thought, and he kept wondering about the real God worthy of worship.

وفى الصباح رأى إبراهيم الشمس، فقال لنفسه هذه أكبر من القمر ولها صفات أقوى من القمر، فلا شك أنها هى الإله الذى أبحث عنه، وظل يتفكر فيها حتى غربت الشمس، فتساءل إبراهيم كيف تكون الشمس إلهاً وتختفى عند الغروب، وظل يتفكر ويبحث عن الإله الحقيقى المستحق للعبادة.

During his search for the one true God,
Allah revealed to Ibrahim the truth:
there is only one God,
the Creator of the whole universe and only He can
help or harm people.
Allah had chosen him, Ibrahim, to deliver His message to his
people and to call them to worship only Allah.

وبعدها هدى الله إبراهيم الى الحقيقة، وهى أن هناك إله واحد خالق السماء والأرض والذى ينفع ويضر. وأختاره الله ليدعو قومه الى عبادة الله وحده.

Ibrahim started his mission to deliver
Allah's message and called on his father
to follow him in worshiping only Allah,
but his father, Azar, didn't believe him.
Azar threatened to throw Ibrahim out of the house
if he were to desert idol worshiping. Ibrahim didn't give up
and tried to convince his father about his true message.

وأبتدأ إبراهيم بدعوة أبيه الى عبادة الله وحده،
ولكن أباه، آذر، كذّب بدعوة إبنه لعبادة الله وحده، بل هدده إن ترك
عبادة آلهة أبائه فإنه سيعاقبه بطرده من البيت.
وحاول إبراهيم مراراً أقناع أبيه بالإيمان بالله وحده.

'He said: "Do you reject my gods,
O Ibrahim? If you don't stop,
I will indeed stone you.
So get away from me safely before I punish you." '
(Maryam: 46)

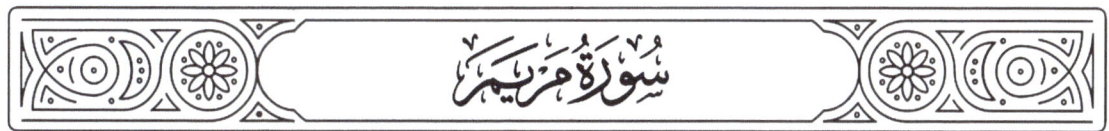

قَالَ أَرَاغِبٌ أَنتَ عَنْ ءَالِهَتِى يَٰإِبْرَٰهِيمُ ۖ لَئِن لَّمْ تَنتَهِ لَأَرْجُمَنَّكَ ۖ وَٱهْجُرْنِى مَلِيًّا ۝

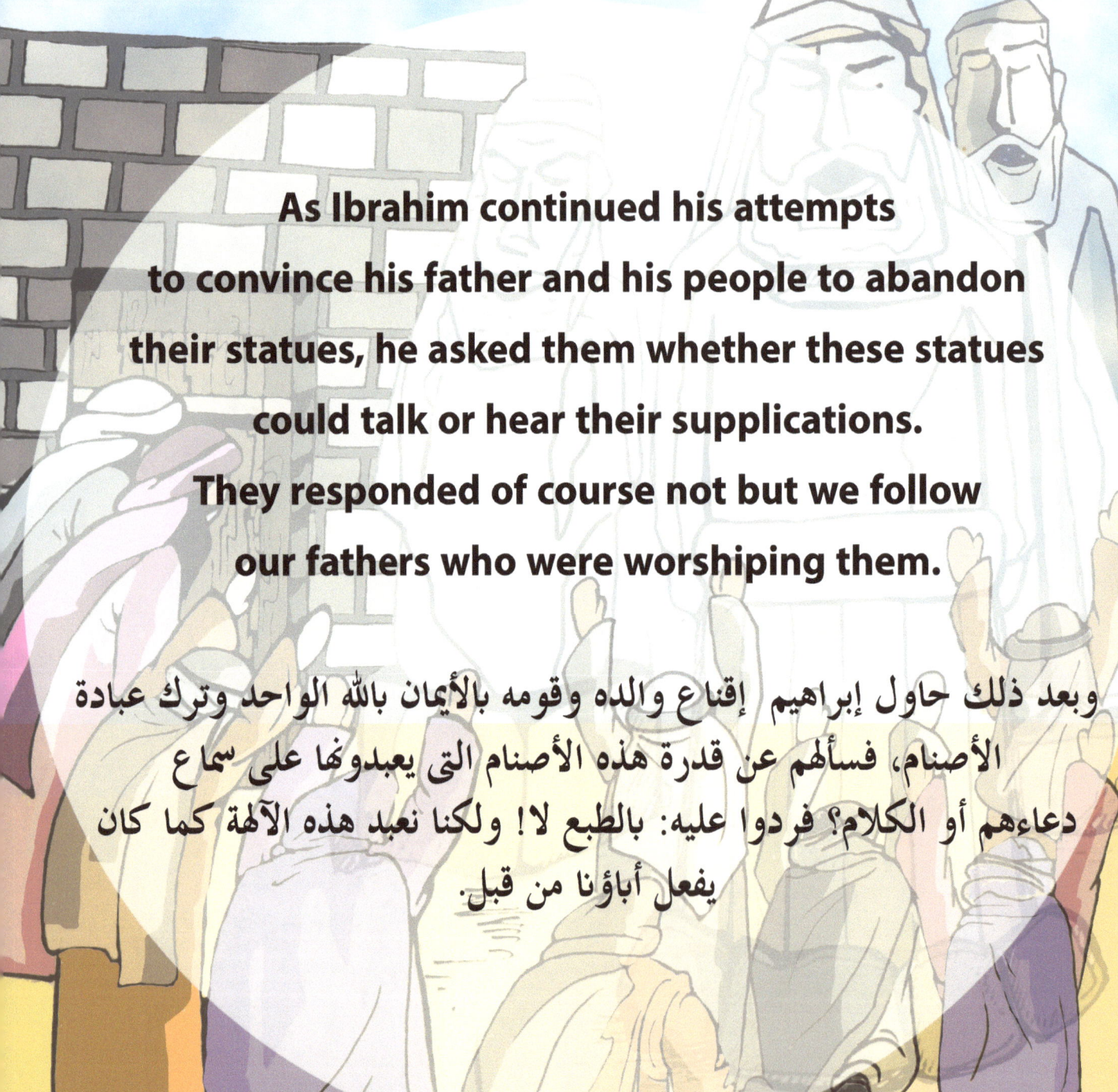

As Ibrahim continued his attempts to convince his father and his people to abandon their statues, he asked them whether these statues could talk or hear their supplications. They responded of course not but we follow our fathers who were worshiping them.

وبعد ذلك حاول إبراهيم إقناع والده وقومه بالإيمان بالله الواحد وترك عبادة الأصنام، فسألهم عن قدرة هذه الأصنام التي يعبدونها على سماع دعائهم أو الكلام؟ فردوا عليه: بالطبع لا! ولكنا نعبد هذه الآلهة كما كان يفعل أباؤنا من قبل.

Ibrahim was surprised at their response.
He thought to himself - how could I worship
any other than Allah Who created me,
provided me with life, food and drink, and health
and strength.

وتعجب إبراهيم من ردهم عليه، فكيف له ألا يعبد الذى خلقه وأحياه، والذى يتولاه بنعمة الطعام والشراب بالإضافة الى الصحة والعافية.

'Who has created me,
and it is He Who guides me, (78)
And it is He Who feeds me and gives
me to drink (79)
And when I am ill, it is He Who cures me, (80)
And Who will cause me to die, and then will bring
me back alive'
(Al-Shuaraa: 78 - 81)

After Ibrahim realized his people will not desert their idols, he waited for an opportunity to be alone with the idols and destroyed all of them with an axe except the biggest one - on which he hung the axe. When the townspeople saw their idols broken into small pieces, they asked Ibrahim who did that to our gods?

ولما لم يجد إبراهيم أي فائدة من تركهم عبادة التماثيل إنتظر حتى تركوه وحيدا مع الأصنام وقام بتكسيرها كلها إلا تمثال منهم وعلق عليه الفأس الذي أستعمله لتكسير التماثيل. ولما عاد قومه رأوا تماثيلهم التي يعبدونها كلها مكسورة إلا واحداً منهم، وتعجبوا من فعل هذا بآلهتهم؟ فأحضروا إبراهيم وسألوه من فعل هذا بآلهتنا؟

'So he broke them to pieces,
except the biggest of them, that they might
turn to it.'

(Al-Anbiya: 58)

He told them their biggest statue was the one who had done it and if they didn't believe him, they could just ask the statue.
His people thought about this and realized that idols couldn't talk.
Ibrahim told them how could you worship something that can't talk, help or hurt you?

فرد عليهم قائلاً إنه كبيرهم هذا المعلق عليه الفأس وتحداهم إن لم يصدقوه أن يسألوا آلهتهم لعلها تدلهم على من قام بتكسير آلهتهم، وعندها أدرك قومه أن هذه الآلهة لا تتكلم، فقال لهم إبراهيم هل يعقل أن تعبدوا تماثيل وتسموها آلهتكم وهي لا تضر ولا تنفع؟

But his people were very arrogant, deceived by their power, and decided to throw Ibrahim into a fire pit as punishment for his daring to destroy their gods.

Allah, of course, would not leave His Messenger alone in this tough situation and ordered the fire to be cool and comfortable for Ibrahim.

ولكن قوم إبراهيم أخذتهم العزة وغرتهم قوتهم وقرروا الإلقاء بإبراهيم في النار عقاباً على جرأته على تكسير آلهتهم، وبالطبع لم يدع الله رسوله في هذا الموقف الصعب، فأمر النار التي أعدها الكفار لإلقائه فيها أن تكون باردة ولا تؤذى إبراهيم.

'They said: "Burn him and help your gods, if you will be doing." (68)
We (Allah) said: "O fire! Be cold and safe for Ibrahim!" '
(Al-Anbiya: 68 - 69)

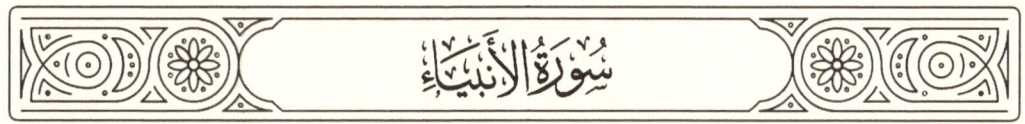

بِسْمِ اللَّهِ الرَّحْمَٰنِ الرَّحِيمِ

قَالُوا حَرِّقُوهُ وَانصُرُوا آلِهَتَكُمْ إِن كُنتُمْ فَاعِلِينَ ﴿٦٨﴾

قُلْنَا يَا نَارُ كُونِي بَرْدًا وَسَلَامًا عَلَىٰ إِبْرَاهِيمَ ﴿٦٩﴾

During his mission to deliver Allah's message, Ibrahim was confronted by a King who did not believe in Allah. When Ibrahim tried to convince the King of the power of Allah to give life and death, the King defied him and tried to show that he too could control life and death. The King had two prisoners brought before him; he killed one of them and freed the other.

وفى أثناء دعوته لعبادة الله وحده، دخل فى مناقشة حادة مع أحد ملوك عصره، فقال إبراهيم فى محاولة إقناع الملك بعبادة الله وحده أن الله هو الذى يحى ويميت، فأمر الملك بإحضار إثنين من المساجين وأمر بإطلاق سراح أحدهما وبقتل الآخر.

Ibrahim was not shaken;
he immediately responded that only Allah
can control the sun.
Allah brings the sun from the East. If you truly claim
to have infinite power so bring the sun from the West!
The King was stunned.

ولكن إبراهيم لم يهتز من رد فعل الملك، وبعدها أتى إبراهيم بدليل دامغ على قدرة الله وقال للملك إن الله يأتي بالشمس من المشرق. فإن كنت كما زعمت عن قدراتك التي لا حدود لها فأتي بالشمس من المغرب، وعندها بُهت الملك.

Ibrahim continued calling
on his people to worship only one God.
He got closer to Allah Who called him
the "Friend of Allah" (or Khalil Allah in Arabic).
Ibrahim didn't have any children and was hopeful to have
progeny to carry on Allah's message.
Even though Ibrahim was getting older, Allah blessed him
with two sons, Ismail and Ishaq.

وبعدها إستمر إبراهيم فى دعوته لعبادة الله وحده، وأزداد تقرباً لله حتى أتخذه الله خليلاً له، ولم يرزق إبراهيم بأولاد له وقد تقدم به السن هو وزوجته، وكانا شديدا الشوق للأولاد حتى يستمروا فى تبليغ الرسالة، فأستجاب له ربه ورزق إبراهيم بإولاد وهما إسماعيل وإسحاق.

One day,
Allah ordered Ibrahim in a dream to sacrifice
his beloved son.
What a tough and difficult way to test Ibrahim!
He asked his son what should he do?
His son was a strong and faithful person, and he replied
if this is a command from Allah then let's do it
and you will find me very patient and obedient.

وفي أحد الأيام، أمر الله إبراهيم في منامه بالتضحية بولده كإمتحان له هل يطيع أمر الله أم يرفض؟ ولقد كان إختباراً شديد الصعوبة، وقد قام إبراهيم بإستشارة إبنه، فرد عليه إبنه بإيمان ثابت وقوى إن كان هذا هو أمر الله فعلينا تنفيذه.

Their faith and trust in Allah
were very strong.
After they both successfully passed Allah's test,
a ram was sent by Allah to be sacrificed in place
of Ibrahim's son.
This event is celebrated by Muslims during Eid al-Adha.

وهكذا بعد أن أثبت إبراهيم وإبنه قوة إيمانهما وثقتهما بالله ونجاحهما في هذا الإختبار الإلهي الصعب أرسل الله كبشاً للتضحية به بدلاً من إبن إبراهيم، وأن تكون هذه المناسبة عيداً للمسلمين.

'He said: "O my son! I have seen in a dream that I offer you in sacrifice to Allah, so look what you think!" He said: "O my father! Do that which you are commanded, Insha Allah, you shall find me of the steadfast." '

(Al-Safaat:102)

فَلَمَّا بَلَغَ مَعَهُ ٱلسَّعْىَ قَالَ يَٰبُنَىَّ إِنِّىٓ أَرَىٰ فِى ٱلْمَنَامِ أَنِّىٓ أَذْبَحُكَ فَٱنظُرْ مَاذَا تَرَىٰ ۚ قَالَ يَٰٓأَبَتِ ٱفْعَلْ مَا تُؤْمَرُ ۖ سَتَجِدُنِىٓ إِن شَآءَ ٱللَّهُ مِنَ ٱلصَّٰبِرِينَ ۝

Allah ordered Ibrahim
and his son Ismail to build the Kaaba,
the Sacred House of Allah, and specified its place.
After building the House of Allah in Makkah,
it became a place where people gather for pilgrimage and
trade from everywhere on Earth.

وقد أمر الله إبراهيم وإبنه إسماعيل أن يقوما ببناء الكعبة بمكة بعد أن حدد لهما مكانها، وبعد أن قاما ببناء الكعبة أصبحت مقراً للحج والمكان الذى يأتى إليه البشر للحج والتجارة من كل مكان فى الأرض.

During his mission to deliver Allah's message, Ibrahim got worried that his people continued to deny His message. They did not believe in Allah's ability to revive the dead on the Day of Judgement. He asked Allah to cleanse his heart from any doubt and provide him with concrete proof.

وأثناء قيام إبراهيم بدعوة قومه لعبادة الله وحده تسرب القلق الى قلبه لإستمرارهم فى رفض دعوته وتكذيبهم لقدرة الله على إحياء الموتى، فطلب من الله أن يريه قدرته على إحياء الموتى ليس لعدم إيمانه بالله ولكن لتثبيته على الإيمان.

Allah told Ibrahim to bring four different birds, to cut them into pieces, to mix them well, then to spread these mixed pieces on various hills, and then to call the birds to come to him. Ibrahim thought this was impossible, how could dead and cut pieces from different birds come back to life! But with Allah's Power and Will, the four birds flew back to Ibrahim.

فأمره الله أن يأتي بأربعة طيور مختلفة الأنواع وأن يقطعهن إلى أجزاء ويخلطهن بلا أي ترتيب، وأن يفرق هذه الأجزاء على عدة جبال، وبعدها أمرالله إبراهيم أن يدعو الطيور. وبالطبع لا يتوقع أي شخص أن الطيور ستستجيب لدعاء إبراهيم، ولكن بقدرة الله ومشيئته عادت الطيور طائرة بين يدي إبراهيم.

Allah has honored Ibrahim
by making all prophets after him from
his progeny. Ibrahim is known as the
"Father of the Prophets".
Among those prophets are Yaqub, Yusuf, Musa, Issa,
and Muhammad (peace be upon them).
Ibrahim emphasized to his sons the importance of sticking to
the religion of Allah and to worship Him alone.

وقد كرم الله عبده إبراهيم بأن جعل الأنبياء من بعده أن يكونوا من سلالته،
ومن بينهم يعقوب ويوسف وموسى وعيسى ومحمد عليهم السلام.
ولهذا عرف إبراهيم ب "أبو الأنبياء"
وقد قام إبراهيم بالتأكيد على أولاده بالتمسك بدين الله
وأن يعبدوا الله وحده.

'And this submission to Allah was enjoined by Ibrahim upon his sons and by Yaqub, "O my sons! Allah has chosen for you the true religion, then die not except in a state of full submission to Allah" '
(Al-Baqara: 132)

وَوَصَّىٰ بِهَآ إِبْرَٰهِـۧمُ بَنِيهِ وَيَعْقُوبُ يَٰبَنِيَّ إِنَّ ٱللَّهَ ٱصْطَفَىٰ لَكُمُ ٱلدِّينَ فَلَا تَمُوتُنَّ إِلَّا وَأَنتُم مُّسْلِمُونَ ۝

THE STORY OF IBRAHIM PBUH HAS MANY LESSONS FOR US TO REMEMBER:

- Reflect and contemplate on the universe around us.

- Be gentle and respectful with your parents.

- Be patient and don't give up easily.

- Put your faith and trust in Allah, especially when facing challenges.

قصة سيدنا إبراهيم تحتوى على عديد من الدروس منها:

- التأمل والتفكر في الكون من حولنا.

- معاملة والدينا بلطف وإحترام.

- التحلى بالصبر وعدم اليأس بسهولة.

- التحلي بالإيمان والثقة بالله خاصة عند مواجهة المصاعب.

Watch a special reading of Ibrahim PBUH by the author!

Scan this QR code to access the video.

www.ingramcontent.com/pod-product-compliance
Lightning Source LLC
Chambersburg PA
CBHW050741110526
44590CB00002B/47